Speak

HEAVEN IS VOICE ACTIVATED

USE THE POWER OF YOUR WORDS TO ACTIVATE
THE CREATIVE WILL OF GOD IN YOUR LIFE

Amy Walton

Dedication

To my beloved husband, Marcus- Thank you for always being there. Your quiet strength, unwavering support, and steady presence have carried me through more than words can express. You are a gift from God, and I'm forever grateful.

To my amazing sons, Rashaad and Rajai- You are my joy, my legacy, and living proof that God answers prayers. May you always speak life, walk boldly in your calling, and know that your words carry the power of Heaven.

With all my love,

Amy Walton

Dear Faith-Filled Believer,

During the next 7 days, we are going to activate the words of our mouth! Did you know the power to change your life lies in your mouth?

Matthew 15:11 says it like this: *"the power of life and death is in the tongue"* Think about it! Our words build up...or they tear down. Either way, the spoken word gets results.

It is easy to feel disheartened when you think about the words you allow to come out of your mouth, but the purpose of this book is to enlighten you and help you change what you say!

Table of Contents

Introduction

Let There Be Light

"Let there be light," and there was light (Genesis 1:3).

Do you know how powerful your words are? Probably not. Therefore, I want to give you insight into the power of your words. Your words are so powerful. They have the ability to take nothing and create something. How do I know this? Well, in the beginning, the Spirit of God hovered over and spoke to the earth, which was without form and void. He called into existence that which did not exist. God spoke and it manifested. If you don't believe me, look at Genesis 1:3, God said, *"Let there be light," and there was light*. He went on to say in verse 6, *"let there be an expanse between the waters, separating water from water," And it was so*. This demonstration of the power of words did not happen just once, but numerous times throughout the Bible. God spoke and everything He spoke all happened indeed.

He used the above Scriptures to call the world and everything in it into existence, and He commands us to do the same. In other words, this is an attribute we got from God as His children – the power to create and make things happen with words. Apparently, words are activators and there is hardly anything that is not associated with them. We need them to communicate effectively both physically and spiritually. We need words to disseminate information; whether written or spoken. More so, our words have the power to heal, to hurt, to bring peace, to cause tumult, to either break or soothe the heart. In other words, we need to use our words carefully if they must produce positive results, because they are indeed powerful. Words have the capacity to either make or mar, build or destroy, etc. The power of words cannot be overemphasized and true wisdom in life is to use the right words for every situation.

Additionally, the words we speak are reflections of who we are, as the Scripture says," *the mouth speaks out of the abundance of the heart.*" Likewise you cannot speak differently from the things you have in your heart. Since the heart is where everything we say originate from, I urge you to be careful and conscious about what you allow in there.

Framing Your World with the Word of God

By faith, we understand that the universe has been framed by the word of God, so that what is seen has not been made out of things which are visible (Hebrews 11:3 WEB).

Words are so powerful that God spoke the world into existence by the creative power of His words (Hebrews 11:3). Each time God spoke, the Holy Ghost acted on the words He spoke and caused what God had commanded to come forth. Interestingly, it is God's will for us to replicate his template on spoken words, because we have the right to, as people who are created in his image and likeness. All we need to do is take full advantage of God's powerful word to frame our world. The amount of goodness you get to enjoy out of life has a lot to do with how positive your words are. In other words, if your life does not have the right amount of goodness, it therefore means that you are not speaking the right words into your life frequently. Hence, it is expedient you unlearn the act of speaking negatively, rather teach yourself how to speak optimism and positivity each time you make the decision to speak.

One truth that we need to realize is that our words are equally as important as our prayers. In fact, for me, speaking the right words complement our prayers to a large extent, while speaking negatively nullify prayers. This is mostly because they are two powerful elements, we can make use of in order to frame our world, recreate our lives as well as circumstances. So, when you are upset, angry, stressed or tensed and you are tempted to speak carelessly, I encourage you to keep mute, instead of speaking words that will be in no way beneficial. Someone once said that words are like eggs, they cannot be gathered back once broken. Likewise, when a wrong or negative statement is made, the effect or impact cannot be reversed or undone. Hence, I urge you to frame your world and everything else around you with God's word. The Holy Ghost who caused all of God's words to spring forth into manifestation is still very much available to make the words you speak happen.

Guard Your Heart

*Above all else, guard your heart, for everything
you do flows from it* (Proverbs 4:23).

It is so important for you to guard your heart because one hundred percent of life's issues flow from it. More so, it is the spiritual center for life. It houses the unconscious, subconscious, conscious thoughts, feelings, beliefs, as well as the will and conscience. The heart contains more than what we are aware of. The way you use your words are dependent on what you have in your heart. You cannot speak more than what is in your heart because your words are a reflection of your thoughts which produce your actions.

You will find stored in your heart are all the images and beliefs you have encountered and accepted during the course of your life. These pictures and ideas resonate within you, influencing your mental, physical, and spiritual health. You will notice that before any words flow out of your mouth, they would have been premeditated in your heart. The heart otherwise referred to as the wellspring of life is the store house that harbors our thoughts, emotions, the things that motivate and mold us. The heart also known as our thought life is so important that King Solomon told his son to guard his heart with all diligence; for out of it are the issues of life. Solomon admonished his son with these words, because he understood that our thought life controls the rest of our being. This is evidently the reason Proverbs 23:7 says, *"As a man thinketh in his heart, so is he"*

So you will agree with me when I tell you that your thought life controls you. Your thoughts - negative, positive, bad or good, —control every of your attitudes which is the sum total of all your thoughts. Our attitudes lead to our actions, this is clearly why it is important we guard our hearts jealously - like your life depends on it, because it actually does.

Jesus also said it is out of the heart that the mouth speaks. Therefore, healing has to take place in the heart for the mouth to speak properly. Healing can happen by speaking the word of God. In Mathew 8:8, the centurion told Jesus to speak the word only and his servant would be healed. If

Jesus could speak the word and someone off in the distance was healed. Then all you have to do is speak the word and your heart will be healed. When your heart is healed, guard it. It is the wellspring of your life. The devil attacks believers by bringing strange thoughts into our heart, and it would be our responsibility not to let those thoughts stay. When the devil sends thoughts into your heart, you don't have to speak them out, for *"thoughts unspoken die unborn."* Rather, speak words of God to cancel the thoughts like the Scripture says in 2 Corinthians 10:5. You cannot fight thoughts with thoughts, but with words. So, when there is a thought not conforming to God in your heart, you should speak the word of God against it.

It is Finished

When Jesus died on the cross, satan was defeated. Jesus said, "It is finished" (John 19:30) and His mission was completed. Now, because of the finished work of Christ we live from a place of victory. We do not work to be blessed. We are blessed because of the death, burial, and resurrection of Christ.

There are seven declarations written for each day of the week. We are using our voice to declare what has already been settled in heaven.

When you speak these prophetic declarations each day, you are activating heaven on your behalf. You are bringing down to earth what God has already done for you in heaven. God's will shall be done in your life. Your voice with God's word will make way for His truths to manifest in your life. You are sending forth the word and the word of God cannot return void. Isaiah 55:11 says so *my word that goes out from my mouth; It will not return to me empty, but will accomplish what I desire and achieve the purpose for which I sent it.* The word of God always produces great results.

Activation

The word of God does not come to pass automatically without being activated. It's like the engine of a car that is in place and functioning properly, nevertheless if it is not ignited, the engine won't come alive. The word of God is like the engine, while your mouth is the activation key. God's words are not just there, they are there for our benefits. But these Kingdom benefits won't be activated until we speak the word - God's word. There lots of promises in the Scriptures for every aspect of life, but we need to activate them before they will become effective. God's word says in John 6:63, *the words that I speak to you they are spirits and they are life.* The only extra thing you need to do is to apply a little faith to hasten a performance of it. However, God's word has been known to be efficacious, effective and potent even without an iota of faith applied to the situation. Put differently, God's word works even when you are speaking it, yet you do not even have much faith in what you are saying. The mere fact that it is God's word is more than enough to bring a performance.

Unfortunately, devil knows the power of confessing God's word, hence the reason he tries so hard to stop you and I from doing this, especially on the regular. The steps to activating God's word is to first know what the Scripture says - when you know scriptures then you will you get to understand that God's word works wonders. Secondly, you get to discover for yourself that there is a scripture for every need or situation. The Bible is filled with numerous promises of God, that are just waiting to be activated by a believer.

And it is so easy to activate heaven on your behalf. All you have to do is open your mouth and speak the word of God. Your voice has a sound that all of heaven knows. When your sound is combined with the word of God heaven responds. Angels are commanded to respond to the sound of God's voice, so it doesn't matter who speaks the word, as long as it is God's word, all the forces of heaven move and work together to bring it to pass. You don't have to wait for your pastor or anointed men of God to speak, before you do. As a child of God, you have direct access to the Father, and when you speak His words, He responds just the way He would have responded to Jesus. Whenever Jesus was to pray in the scriptures, He would first give thanks to God, saying *"Father, I thank you that you have heard me. I knew that you always hear me, but I said this on account of the people standing around, that they may believe that you sent me."* (John 11:41-42) Jesus was always confident that God would hear Him when He speaks, and you must have that kind of confidence when you declare God's words. You should be so assured that when you speak God's words back to Him, He would hear you.

When you speak God's words, you're giving your angels what to work with on your behalf. But if you do not speak, they are just there with nothing to do. They are only commanded to obey the voice of His word. (Psalm 103:20). So, when you speak words that are not of God, they are forced to return back to God, that the individual they have been assigned to, is not speaking the words they can work with. Now, speaking God's word is not the same as complaining. Confession does not equal complaining.

When you complain, you're downgrading the power of God in your life, because complaining means you don't trust what God has said in His words enough to confess it.

God is not moved by your complaints or your tears, He is moved by His words in your mouth. All He requires of you is to speak His words with faith. This is so funny because He has already said those words, but He still needs you to speak them back to Him in your own words. He said in Isaiah 1:18, *"Come now, let us reason together,"* He can do anything He wishes to do without having to reason with man, but He chose to call man to reason together with Him. He can bring His words to pass without the involvement of man, but He wouldn't do that, He wants you to speak the words to manifestation. Confession is also different from positive affirmations, although they are better than speaking negative. However, God answers to His words, not words of your culture or environment. As long as you can find them in the scriptures, then you can be sure that God will honor His words.

Each day make these declarations with boldness and authority. It only takes a few minutes each day. It is so simple even a child can do it. You can make these prophetic declarations several times during the course of your day. Every time you make a declaration, you are sending God, who is the word, on assignment. God never fails. He is the guarantee for a great outcome.

When you make your prophetic declarations, don't forget to include your family and friends. Speak the word over them and watch the word of God prosper them. It is impossible to speak God's word without getting outstanding results.

Are you ready? Let's go!

Romans 4:17b says "*... and calls into existence the things that do not exist,*" In other words, you should keep confessing the word till the situation around you changes.

Day One

1. God, I exalt and praise you for the wonderful things you have done in my life (Isaiah 25:1)

2. I am fearfully and wonderfully made and I know that fully well (Psalm 139:14)

3. I am abundantly blessed (Psalm 132:15).

4. I am not afraid, I have power, love, and self-discipline (2 Timothy 1:7)

5. I am anxious for nothing, but in everything by prayer and supplication with thanksgiving I let my requests be made known to God. And the peace of God, which surpasses all comprehension, will guard my hearts and minds in Christ Jesus (Philippians 4:6-7).

6. I am a crown of glory and a royal diadem in the hand of the LORD (Isaiah 62:3).

7. Daily, God loads me up with benefits. He is my salvation (Psalm 68:19).

8. The Lord is my confidence and He will keep me safe and sound (Proverbs 3:26)

9. I will not be defeated because God perfects those things which concerns me (Psalm 138:8)

10. I am not conformed to the patterns of this world but I am transformed by the renewing of my mind that I may prove what is that good, acceptable, and perfect will of God (Romans 12:2)

Day Two

1. I will glorify the Lord and exalt His name (Psalm 34:3)

2. I am created in the image and likeness of God (Genesis 1:26)

3. Set a watch, O Lord, before my mouth and keep the doors of my lips (Psalm 141:3)

4. I am fully persuaded that what God has promised me, he is able to perform (Romans 4:21)

5. I can do all things through Christ who gives me strength (Philippians 4:13)

6. I will seek first the kingdom of God and his righteousness and everything I need will be added to me (Matthew 6:33)

7. I am strong in the Lord and the power of His might so I will not be defeated (Ephesians 6:10-11)

8. I experience the love of Christ and the fullness of life and power that comes from God (Ephesians 3:19)

9. God chose me and appointed me to go out and bear fruit that last! (John 15:16)

10. I am not conformed to the patterns of this world but I am transformed by the renewing of my mind that I may prove what is that good, acceptable, and perfect will of God (Romans 12:2)

Day Three

1. I will exalt you, O Lord, and worship at your footstool; for you are holy (Psalm 99:5)

2. I am the light of the world and the salt of the earth (Matthew 5:13-16)

3. I am the apple of God's eye and He instructs me (Zechariah 2:8).

4. I am the righteousness of God in Christ Jesus (2 Corinthians 5:21)

5. I will not let corrupt communication come out of my mouth, only words that edify those who listen to me (Ephesians 4:29)

6. My times are in your hands, Lord and you deliver me from the hands of my enemies and those who pursue me (Psalm 31:15)

7. I cast down imagination and every high thing that exalts itself against the knowledge of God and bring every thought captive to the obedience of Christ (2 Corinthians 10:5)

8. I will not cast away my confidence, knowing that it will have great recompense of reward (Hebrews 10:35)

9. My prayers are powerful and effective (James 5:16)

10. I am not conformed to the patterns of this world but I am transformed by the renewing of my mind that I may prove what is that good, acceptable, and perfect will of God (Romans 12:2)

Day Four

1. Oh, I give thanks to the lord for He is good; His love endures forever (1 Chronicles 16:34)

2. The Lord is on my side and I will not fear what man can do to me (Psalm 118:6)

3. I declare that no weapon formed against me shall prosper and every tongue that rises against me in judgment I shall condemn for this is the heritage of the saints and my vindication is from the Lord (Isaiah 54: 17)

4. I will forget the former things and not dwell on things of old. God is doing a new thing in my life (Isaiah 43:18-19)

5. God is able to make all grace abound toward me and I have sufficiency in all things (2 Corinthians 9:8)

6. The Lord shall bless me and keep me; He shall make His face to smile upon me, be gracious to me and give me peace (Numbers 6:24-25)

7. I have the Spirit of wisdom and revelation that I may know God better. The eyes of my understanding are enlightened that I may know the hope of His calling,

the glorious riches of His inheritance among the saints (Ephesians 1:17-18)

8. I am seated in heavenly place, far above every ruler and authority, power and dominion, and every title given, not only in this age but also in the one to come. Everything is under my feet and I am head over everything for the church (Ephesians 1:20-22)

9. My ears are open and I hear what the Spirit of the Lord is saying to me (Revelation 2:7)

10. I am not conformed to the patterns of this world but I am transformed by the renewing of my mind that I may prove what is that good, acceptable, and perfect will of God (Romans 12:2).

Day Five

1. This is the day which the Lord hath made, I will rejoice and be glad in it (Psalm 118:24)
2. My mouth is a fountain of life (Proverbs 10:11)
3. I am strengthened with all power according to His might. I have great endurance and patience (Colossians 1:11)
4. I press on to take hold of that which Christ Jesus took hold of me. Forgetting those things which are behind and reaching forward to those things which are ahead, I press toward the goal for the prize of the upward call of God in Christ Jesus (Philippians 3:12-14).
5. The glory of the Lord is upon me and I will rise above every test or trial that comes my way (Isaiah 60:1)
6. I am kind, tenderhearted forgiving others as God in Christ has forgiven me (Ephesians 4:32).
7. God makes all grace abound toward me so that I always have all sufficiency and an abundance for every good work (2 Corinthians 9:8).

8. The LORD opens to me His good treasure, the heavens to give the rain to my land in its season and to bless all the work of my hand (Deuteronomy 28:12).

9. I am blessed and favor surrounds me like a shield (Psalm 5:12).

10. I am not conformed to the patterns of this world but I am transformed by the renewing of my mind that I may prove what is that good, acceptable, and perfect will of God (Romans 12:2)

Day Six

1. I will bless the Lord at all times and His praise shall be continually in my mouth (Psalm 34:1)

2. I walk in a manner worthy of the Lord, pleasing Him in all respects. I bear fruit in every good work and I am increasing in the knowledge of God (Colossians 1:10)

3. I am a servant of God and He takes pleasure in my prosperity (Psalm 35:27)

4. My ways please the LORD and He makes even my enemies to be at peace with me (Proverbs 16:7)

5. The joy of the LORD is my strength (Nehemiah 8:10).

6. I am the head and not the tail

7. God works in me both to will and to do His good pleasure (Philippians 2:13)

8. God satisfies my mouth with good things and renews my youth like the eagles' (Psalm 103:5).

9. The fruit of my womb is blessed, produce of the ground, the increase of my herds, my cattle, and the offspring of my flock (Deuteronomy 28:4).

10. I am not conformed to the patterns of this world but I am transformed by the renewing of my mind that I may prove what is that good, acceptable, and perfect will of God (Romans 12:2).

Day Seven

1. I will exalt you, my God the King; I will praise your name for ever and ever (Psalm 145:1)

2. I am confident of this very thing, that He who has begun a good work in me will complete it until the day of Jesus Christ (Philippians 1:6).

3. God redeems my life from the pit. He crowns me with lovingkindness and compassion (Psalm 103:4)

4. I am anxious for nothing, but in everything by prayer and supplication with thanksgiving I let my requests be made known to God. And the peace of God, which surpasses all comprehension, will guard my hearts and minds in Christ Jesus (Philippians 4:6-7).

5. I think on whatever is true, noble, just, pure, lovely, and of good report, if anything is excellent or praiseworthy I think about these things (Philippians 4:8).

6. I am more than a conqueror through Him who loved me (Romans 8:37)

7. I can quench all the fiery darts of the wicked one with my shield of faith (Ephesians 6:16)

8. I am God's workmanship, created in Christ unto good works (Ephesians 2:10).

9. I am an overcomer by the blood of the Lamb and the word of my testimony (Revelation 12:11).

10. I am not conformed to the patterns of this world but I am transformed by the renewing of my mind that I may prove what is that good, acceptable, and perfect will of God (Romans 12:2)

Conclusion

Whenever God speaks a word, the power to accomplish it immediately goes with the word. Like the scripture says that not a jot of His word will go unfulfilled. Every word that is regarded as God's word possess the power to come to pass. When God says it; it has to happen. When Jesus died, He gave us His name, His word and His spirit. The Bible is God's word to us and like Joshua said, it has to consistently be in our mouths. God's word can be the written word of God (the Bible) or the spoken word of God (through the Holy Spirit to our spirits or through His prophets). *"The word of God is sharper than any two edged sword"*, (Hebrews 4:12). God's word brings a deep conviction and brings deep understanding of all things. It is a light that unravels mysteries, bringing light and understanding to certain issues.

God's word has to become flesh for it to manifest in the physical. John says Jesus Himself is the word and He now lives inside of us through the infilling of the Holy Spirit and consistent meditation of the scriptures. His words have the power to bring healing to the sick, save the sinners, edify the saints, freedom to the bound and deliverance to the oppressed. The word spoken by God is spiritual and it needs to mix with our faith, works and words to become physical. You cannot enjoy the word as it were, if it does not become flesh to you.

If you apply the word of God and believe in its potency, you will have results from the word. The word works, you only need to work it out. When God sends His word on a particular situation, it is settled in the spirit realm and there is no limit to the power and potency of that word. But man can limit the manifestation because it depends on so many things, like faith, consistency in confessing the word and the words we say after God has spoken. Many a times, we claim to believe what God has said, but our own words do not conform to the words of God. And God's word will not work for you if you are saying contradictory words. Your actions must also conform to the words of God you're confessing. If God's word says you're healed, then you have to act like the healed. If He says none shall be barren in the land, then your actions must show that you are not acting like the barren. The goal to enjoying God's word come to pass in our lives is to act like it is so, even before we see the physical manifestation.

You will also decree a thing, and it will be established for you; And light will shine on your ways. (Job 22:28)

If you are ready to change your life, then it's time to change your words. Sowing a different seed allows you to reap a different harvest. Begin now, speaking life over you and your future. Let your words speak for you. Declare I am blessed. Everything that I touch is blessed. I can have what God says I can have. I can do what God says I can do. I am blessed going and blessed coming. The fruit of my womb is blessed. I am the head and not the tail. I am victorious. There is power in your words. Choose them carefully. Speak life, choose life, and you and your house will live.

Prayer

Dear Heavenly Father, I repent for speaking words of death and defeat. I ask that you help me to speak life so that I am victorious in every area of my life in Jesus name, Amen.

Holy Spirit, help me to always speak and activate God's words in my life and affairs in the name of Jesus. I declare that the blessings and the covenants of God for me in the scriptures come to pass, and I walk in the manifestation of them. I act like it is so because God has said so. My actions and words conform to what God has said. I cancel every negative word that I have said concerning myself, my family, my career and my business.

My thoughts are sanctified and purified to think only the things of God. My mind is renewed by the word of God, as I take action to constantly study, meditate, and speak God's words. I decree that only the words of the Lord come to fulfilment in my life. I pray that I will not be ensnared by the words of my mouth.

The Lord will help me and keep a watch over my mouth, so that I will not speak words of death. The angels assigned to me will have assignments to do because I speak words that they can work with on my behalf. I speak words of life, words of encouragement, words of hope to those around me. Through my words, men will be saved and delivered. My words bring healing and give Glory to God, the Father. In Jesus name, Amen.

About the Author

Dr. Amy Walton, affectionately known as "Dr. Amy," is an esteemed prophetic teacher, speaker, coach, and catalyst for change, specializing in guiding Christians on their journey of faith. With a deep passion for empowering individuals to overcome obstacles hindering spiritual growth, she inspires others to live authentically while nurturing a strong connection to their faith. Beyond her professional endeavors, she cherishes her roles as a devoted wife to Marcus and a nurturing mother to Rashaad and Rajai. As an ordained minister of the Gospel of Jesus Christ, she spreads the transformative power of the Good News, impacting countless lives with her message of hope and renewal. Dr. Amy Walton's unwavering commitment to empowering spiritual growth is a testament to her sincere dedication and heartfelt desire to see lives positively transformed.

To Connect:

Website: wwwdramywalton.com

Facebook: Facebook.com/DrAmyWalton

Instagram: dramywalton

Clubhouse: Dr Amy Walton